LIES WE TELL OURSELVES:
THE PSYCHOLOGY OF SELF-DECEPTION

Lies We Tell Ourselves: The Psychology Of Self-Deception
by Cortney S. Warren, Ph.D. - Copyright © 2014
Published by Insight Publishing
Cover by Steve Wilson
Formatting & Layout by Chris Ott

Printed in the United States of America
ISBN 978-061599-771-1

TABLE OF CONTENTS

ACKNOWLEDGEMENTS

This book is written with deep gratitude for the countless individuals who have helped me become more honest with myself. Family, friends, students, patients, colleagues, mentors, and acquaintances: whether our interactions were easy or hard, loving or tense, fleeting or long-term, I thank you for helping me on my journey.

I also want to acknowledge some of the great pioneers in psychology whose theories laid the foundation for the practice of psychotherapy: Sigmund Freud, Carl Jung, Alfred Adler, Fritz Perls, Carl Rogers, Albert Ellis, Aaron Beck, Viktor Frankl, and Irvin Yalom. I could not have written this book without their contributions to the field and to my development as a clinical psychologist.

Most importantly, this book is dedicated to my daughter, Isabella Rose, who helped me become more honest than anyone else in my life.

My friend and colleague, Dr. Andrea Goeglein, recently asked me a very provocative question: "If you gave a fifteen-minute talk about psychology to the public, what would you say and why?"

It seemed to be an easy enough question. I thought about it. I could give a talk on the ways that mainstream American culture breeds unhealthy eating behavior and dissatisfaction with our appearance. Or, I could give a talk on cultural competency and the ways that we struggle to navigate differences related to race, sex, class, sexual orientation, and a host of other socially taboo topics. These are my primary areas of expertise and themes that I have been formally researching for the last two decades. Although they would be easy for me to do, neither felt right.

As I thought more deeply, I considered the bigger picture. I thought about the fundamental importance of psychology as a field, which I believe is to help us understand ourselves. I thought about teaching students the basic principles of psychotherapy, diversity in psychology, and issues related to mental health and illness. I thought about the patients that I have had the honor of treating during the last fifteen years. I thought about my own personal life—my relationships, family dynamics, personality, and the core issues that I navigate. Across these experiences, what is a common thread that would be important to everyone? What can I tell people that could really enhance their ability to live a more fulfilling life?

A topic started forming in my mind, accompanied by a subtle nagging discomfort: *we teach what we most need to learn.* Like most important information worth sharing, this is a topic that most of us struggle with on a daily basis—myself included. *Self-deception.* The answer was clear: I would give a talk on how we lie to ourselves, why it is a problem, and how to start the journey of knowing ourselves by choosing to be more honest. For only when we are honest with ourselves do we have the opportunity to change.

"That is it!" she said. "Now will you please submit a proposal to give a TEDx talk on that topic? TED distributes *Ideas Worth Spreading,* information that can change the world. That is the talk you need to give. That is the talk we need to hear."

Although I had no intention of giving a talk on lying or writing a book about self-deception, the ideas presented in this book took me years to articulate. I wrote this book for people committed to being more honest with themselves. In it, I detail what I see as the truth about human nature in hopes that you can use this information to live a more fulfilling life. If this material causes discomfort in the short-term, know that I believe it will benefit you greatly in the long-term.

PART I: SELF-DECEPTION AND LYING

Humans are excellent liars. We don't like to think of ourselves as capable of lying; it hurts us too much to admit. So we lie to ourselves about that, too.

As a clinical psychologist, I am regularly confronted with the brutal truth that we all lie. I am not talking about deliberate, bold-faced lying, although research suggests that most of us do that on a daily basis. No, this type of dishonesty is far harder to detect and admit. It is the kind of lying that comes from not being psychologically strong enough to be honest with ourselves about who we are. And I believe that it is our biggest obstacle to living a fulfilling life.

I was in graduate school when I started really delving into the topic of self-deception. At the most basic level, self-deception is fooling ourselves into believing something that is false —or— not believing something that is true. As I started intentionally observing myself and my environment, I was shocked; I saw self-deception *everywhere,* in *everyone.*

My own life was riddled with examples. Nowhere were they more obvious than in my romantic relationships. I was attracted to men who were emotionally unavailable, non-committal, and embodied the "ideal" in some way; they were very handsome or athletic, very rich or smart. In these relationships, I was terrified of being abandoned. My fear led me to act in ways that are *still* hard for me to admit: anxiously awaiting a phone call or postcard; driving to see if he was where he said he would be; asking him repeatedly if he loved or missed me; looking for subtleties in his behavior as evidence that he might leave. When I dated men who were emotionally available, I felt suffocated and I eventually left. Of course, I couldn't have told you any of this at the time because *I wouldn't have been able to admit it to myself.* Looking at me from the outside, you would have had no idea of my inner experience—I was already an expert at masking my imperfections and vulnerabilities.

The truth is that our self-deceptive lies range from seemingly tiny untruths to massive life-altering falsehoods about reality. We lie to maintain social appropriateness: "Oh yes, we should definitely grab lunch sometime" (although I have no interest in ever seeing you again, *I tell myself that it is okay to lie to you because I don't want to seem rude*). We lie to reflect the aspirational goals that we unconsciously know we will not uphold: "I will only have one glass of wine tonight" (*when I know full-well that I am having at least three*). We lie to uphold social ideals: "I never have sexual thoughts about anyone except my spouse" (*because that wouldn't be acceptable*).

We lie to ourselves about the smallest details, such as acknowledging how much we *really* ate today. And we lie to ourselves about our largest life choices, such as why we got married or chose a given career path. Unfortunately for all of the romantics reading this book, *love* is *rarely* the full motivation for these choices.

What became increasingly obvious to me was that telling ourselves lies—from the miniscule to the enormous—came with *profound consequences* for ourselves, our loved ones, and our communities.

My goal in writing this book is to help us become more honest with ourselves in hopes that we will live more fulfilling lives. As you might imagine, this topic presents me with a serious dilemma: I can't ask you how you deceive yourself because that would require you to tell the truth. Consequently, I present a range of examples couched in psychological theory to be used as a platform to explore yourself. I encourage you to read this book with an open mind; read it as if a part of every piece of material presented is relevant to you and your life in some way. For it is only when we acknowledge who we really are that we have the opportunity to change.

THE MAKING OF A LIAR

Children learn more from what you are than from what you teach.
—W. E. B. Dubois

It is hard to look at a tiny, innocent little baby and think "liar." But the truth is that from a very young age we start absorbing information that will influence our ability to be honest with ourselves. By observing and experiencing our environment, we start to learn what is acceptable and unacceptable, desirable and undesirable—and soon, what is *true* and *untrue* of us.

I want you to think about yourself as a child. Many things influenced your development—your parents, siblings, friends, favored activities, school, the media, the collective values of your culture. If you think back, you can probably identify some situations that were objectively hard for you, perhaps even those as extreme as emotional, sexual, or physical abuse. You can also identify more subtle nuances of your environment, such as the way that your parent talked to you and the buttons that you knew you shouldn't ever push. All of these experiences—the seemingly big to the seemingly small—taught you something. What you learned will give you a great deal of information about *areas in which you will be vulnerable to self-deception.* Below are some examples to consider.

- Perhaps you learned not to talk about your step-family in front of your mother because it was clear from her behavior that she was uncomfortable with the topic. You learned to systematically edit yourself before speaking to ensure that you didn't offend. In fact, you hid entire parts of your life to protect her from discomfort.

- Perhaps you learned that it is more important to uphold the family image (of perfection, nobility, positivity) than to be honest about its flaws.

- Perhaps you grew up in a single-parent home in which you were neglected by your father: he only spent time with you when it was convenient for him. You thought that meant something was wrong with you—you were not smart enough, attractive enough, athletic enough. Consequently, to win his love and hide your flaws from others, you learned that you needed to be perfect—not to show any negative traits to anyone, to hide them at all costs. Otherwise, people would leave you.

7

- Perhaps you grew up in an environment in which you felt ugly. You thought your friends were better looking than you and you looked nothing like the models on television. You learned that you were less valuable than they were and found comfort in eating.

- Perhaps your home environment was generally happy and healthy. You loved your parents and saw that they worked hard to support you. Consequently, you couldn't acknowledge anything negative about your upbringing; it felt as though you were disrespecting your family. You learned that to say something negative—even if it were true—dismissed the positive.

- Perhaps you learned that it is easier to believe people will change than to admit that they may not.

- Perhaps you were teased and criticized by your peers. This made you bitter and angry at the world because you felt so misunderstood. You learned that it is easier to reject others before they mistreat you and to act with an air of superiority to cover up your insecurity about not being accepted.

- Perhaps you learned to value people's intentions more than their actual behavior. When people claim to love you, you value what they tell you rather than the way they treat you.

- Perhaps you grew up in an environment in which expression of negative emotion was punished. If you said that something painful was happening to you or expressed sadness, you were told that you were wrong, you were hit, or you were ignored. Consequently, you learned that expressing negative emotion should be avoided at all costs. You may even deny experiencing negative emotion entirely.

- Perhaps you learned that women would always hurt you.

- Perhaps you were adopted and you were never sure whether your birth parents wanted you, loved you, or cared about what happened to you. At the same time, your adoptive parents catered to your every need for fear that you wouldn't feel loved or love them. Consequently, you learned that you could get away with "bad behavior" if you reminded people that you were adopted and had a challenging life.

- Perhaps you learned that money is bad because it led to so many arguments between your parents. You either didn't have enough or people didn't agree on how to spend it.

- Perhaps you did not have physical or emotional security as a child and developed a paralyzing fear of abandonment. You learned that you were not safe if you were alone.

- Perhaps your father was a member of the armed forces. After serving his country abroad, he came back a changed person—he was traumatized by his experiences but wouldn't talk about it. Instead, he drank and became isolated. As a result, you tried to meet his needs and felt responsible for his well-being. You learned that you should put others' needs before your own.

- Perhaps you learned that if you threw a temper tantrum you would get candy.

- Perhaps your mother was very emotionally volatile. Anything could set her off. One minute she was happy and loving toward you and the next she was angry and resentful that you existed. You learned not to get close to people because they were not trustworthy.

- Perhaps you learned that crying is the best way to get someone to stop yelling at you.

- Perhaps you were the caretaker and peacemaker in your environment. When your sibling was in trouble, you tried to stop the fighting among family members. You learned to avoid conflict to keep the peace, even when expressing your honest feelings would have been beneficial to you and your relationships.

The ways that our childhood environment can affect who we become are endless. What we learn will be very specific to our own life experiences and a variety of personal factors, such as our biology and personality. That said, I cannot overemphasize the impact our childhood has on our ability to be honest because *we live out what we learned as children in our adult relationships.*

Whether what you learned was objectively true or false, the conclusions that you made about yourself, your environment, and other people will be replayed in your life because *they become a part of who you are.* This will happen whether you are aware of it or not. When you are not aware that you are bringing old learning to your current relationships, *you will want to lie about where it is coming from*. For example:

- If you learned that if you are not perfect, people will leave you; you strive to give the appearance of competence at all times at the cost of telling the truth. When someone confronts you with an observation about your imperfections, you will likely feel tremendous anxiety and lie to yourself (and to them) to avoid seeing it.

- If you learned to value people's intentions more than their actual behavior, you will likely make excuses for people who treat you poorly but claim to love you. You may find yourself in a pattern of relationships in which you are taken advantage of, maltreated, or underappreciated. Yet, you will lie to yourself about why you neither leave nor require that they change.

- If you learned that expressing negative emotion should be avoided at all costs, you will likely struggle to manage conflict in your adult relationships because you will lie to yourself about your true feelings.

- If you learned that you were flawed, broken, or unlovable, you may engage in behavior that reflects those beliefs. Perhaps you became a prostitute, drug addict, or high school dropout. You lie to yourself about your potential because you have already concluded that you will not become anything important in life.

- If you learned that money is bad, you will likely struggle to earn and manage money as an adult without understanding why.

- If you learned that you were not safe if you were alone, you will go to great lengths to be in relationships. You may have been married and divorced multiple times or engage in casual sexual relationships to avoid being single. Yet, you will not admit that the reason for your serial relationships is a deep-seated fear of being alone.

- If you learned that it is easier to believe that people will change than that they will stay the same, you may convince yourself to stay in relationships for a long time, even if you are not happy. You lie about the fact that you have absolutely no control over whether your partners change.

- If you learned to systematically edit yourself before speaking to ensure that you don't offend people, you may create a very compartmentalized life. You act one way at work, another way with friends, and a third way with your family at home. You lie about who you really are by showing only the parts of you that you believe are easy for them to accept.

The bottom line is this: The areas in which we felt most insecure, unsafe, unloved, uncomfortable, embarrassed, angry, and generally unresolved as a child are the areas that we will be most prone to self-deception as an adult. For in these areas, we will not want to admit that what we learned as children *affected who we are and is influencing the way we are living our lives as adults.* The more we lie to ourselves about how we are contributing to our problems, the more harm we will cause to ourselves and our relationships because we will blame others for undesirable aspects of our lives instead of taking responsibility for our role.

To illustrate this point, I will end with a personal example. As I shared earlier, self-deception permeated my romantic life. At the time, I knew that I didn't feel safe in my relationships and I knew that I wanted to feel safe. Yet, I believed that it was up to the man in my life to make me feel safe—I thought that if he just called me more often, told me he loved me a few more times, committed to marry me, *then I would feel safe.* These feelings were reflected in my behavior—I blamed him for my feelings and told him repeatedly to change his behavior so that I could feel better. This often left the men in my life feeling belittled, misunderstood, and burdened because nothing they did was good enough—I never felt safe, despite their efforts.

The truth that I could not admit was this: The real reason I didn't feel safe was that I learned as a child that people would always leave me. I also learned to do everything in my power to make them stay because I knew that I wasn't capable of taking care of myself as a child. Consequently, although I blamed the men in my life for not making me feel secure enough in my adult relationships, the truth was that *there was nothing they could do to make me feel safe because my feelings had nothing to do with them.*

In addition, I chose men who would never make me feel safe because they were emotionally unavailable, which was familiar and reflected my greatest insecurities. As such, I was contributing to my own feelings of insecurity through the men I chose to date.

In the end, my self-deception caused me and many well-intentioned men a great deal of pain. I lied to all of us about who I was, where my feelings came from, and how I contributed to our relationship issues. And it all stemmed from my inability to be honest with myself.

The truth is that we can't handle the truth. Self-deception comes from not having enough psychological strength to admit the truth and deal with the consequences that will follow when the truth is acknowledged.

We don't want to see our insecurities, our ugliness, our pained and damaged parts. We don't want to acknowledge painful things that happened to us or the person we became because of our response to challenging life circumstances. When we acknowledge our lies, it forces us to face the parts of ourselves that we don't want to admit.

In this way, our tendency to deceive ourselves is part of human nature. It is actually a good survival strategy to manipulate, twist, and reorganize the truth in a way that is more consistent with what we can psychologically tolerate. It helps us deal with some of the most miserable realities of human life.

Consistent with self-deception as a means of self-preservation, theories of psychological development can help us understand our tendency to lie. In this section, I use some of the most prominent theories of human nature to describe ways we commonly deceive ourselves. As I describe them, I encourage you to think about your use of these lying strategies in your own life. Remember that *all* of us lie to ourselves in these ways, but each of us will use some of these techniques more than others because of our unique backgrounds and learning experiences.

Psychoanalytic/Dynamic Perspective

Being entirely honest with oneself is a good exercise.
—Sigmund Freud

As the founder of psychotherapy, Sigmund Freud is one of the most influential scientists of the last century. While studying medicine at the University of Vienna, Freud began treating women with hysteria, a mental illness characterized by severe symptoms such as paralysis, strong emotional reactions, and hallucinations. What Freud found shocked the medical community; talking to these women made their symptoms less severe. Referred to as *the talking cure*, Freud used these experiences to develop the first comprehensive theory of personality development and started the practice of psychoanalysis—the first therapy.

Through his observations, Freud described the ways that we lie to ourselves through *ego-defense mechanisms*. Freud and many later psychodynamic scholars (including his daughter, Anna) proposed that we use a variety of psychological strategies to protect ourselves from any information that would hurt our *ego*—our core sense of self. Some of the most common of these strategies are the following:

Denial: Lying to ourselves by refusing to acknowledge that something is true *even though it is*. This is any version of "I am not, not, *not* like that," even though your thoughts, feelings, and behavior suggest that you are. Often, the closer you are to the truth, the more strongly you are going to deny it. For example:

- "I do not have a problem with alcohol" (even though I drink every day, sometimes with breakfast).
- "I am not jealous" (even though I secretly check my partner's email and text messages).
- "I am not a cheater" (even though I have cheated in the past).
- "I am not insecure about my looks" (even though I stare at the stunning woman or handsome man walking through the café with the intensity of a hawk).
- "I am a good parent" (even though I scream and swear at my kids when I am upset).
- "I am over him or her" (even though I wait for a phone call, look through old photos, and try to make him or her jealous by very publicly dating another person).

Rationalization: Lying to ourselves by creating a reason to excuse our behavior. For example:

- "I wouldn't have yelled at you if you hadn't treated me so unfairly" (thereby justifying my yelling).
- "If you treat me badly, I will hit you. I am not going to tolerate disrespect from anyone" (thereby justifying my tendency to get in physical fights).
- "I know that smoking isn't good for my health, but it helps me lose weight" (thereby making me feel better about the fact that I smoke).

- "Even though I am on a diet, I can eat this chocolate cake because I ate so well yesterday" (which translates to, "I ate almost nothing yesterday, so I can eat cake today").

Sometimes we even rationalize to cover up other lies. For example, if we cheated on a test, we may say to ourselves, "I didn't have time to study last night. I don't usually cheat, so this is the exception" (thereby telling myself that I am not really a cheater).

Projection: Lying by taking an undesirable aspect of ourselves and ascribing it to someone else. This is any version of "*I* am not like that—*you* are like that." These are often situations in which we look like hypocrites. For example:

- Instead of acknowledging your own struggles with infidelity, you accuse your partner of cheating.
- When dating someone in whom you have lost interest, you say things like, "I don't think you are ready for this relationship," instead of acknowledging that you are not ready for this relationship—and never will be!
- Instead of seeing that you struggle to get emotionally close to people, you accuse your friends of being emotionally unavailable.

Regression: Lying to ourselves by becoming more immature than would be expected for our age. In psychological language, this is reverting to an earlier stage of development. For example:

- Instead of having a mature, adult disagreement, you get into an argument in which you look like you are "throwing a two-year old's temper tantrum."
- When you are angry with someone, you become passive-aggressive by refusing to talk to the person. When you do speak, you say things like, "everything is fine" and "if something *is* wrong, you should know what it is."
- If you do not get what you want, you act like a sulking child.

Displacement: Lying to ourselves by taking our true feelings out on people or objects that are less threatening than the original situation or stimulus. In other words, rather than expressing ourselves in a situation that could have negative consequences (e.g., when dealing with someone in a position of power such as a boss, a parent, a teacher), we express our emotion at people or objects that have less power. For example:

- You have a bad day at work. Instead of acknowledging your emotional struggle at work, you come home and belittle your child, kick the dog, or cause conflict with your spouse.

- You get into an argument with your partner. Instead of processing the content of the disagreement, you go to the bar and get into a fight with another patron.

Existential Perspective

When we are no longer able to change a situation, we are challenged to change ourselves.
—Viktor Frankl

Following the teachings of famous philosophers such as Søren Kierkegaard, Friedrich Nietzsche, and Martin Heidegger, existential psychologists argue that there are four basic facts about being human that we must confront during our lifetimes. As described by prominent figures such as Viktor Frankl and Irvin Yalom, the *Givens of Life* are as follows:

1. You and everyone you love will die.
2. You are ultimately alone housed in a solitary physical body.
3. Your life has no inherent meaning unless you give it meaning because none of us is that significant in the grand scope of human history.
4. You are responsible for who you are, independent of life circumstances, because you have the freedom of choice.

As we confront these life realities, we generally feel anxious and uncomfortable. They are not intended to be harsh–although they may sound it. They are intended to be an accurate reflection of reality that should motivate us to create a more meaningful existence for ourselves.

To cope with these Givens, however, we often resort to self-deception. For example, ask yourself whether you try to avoid the Givens in the following ways:

- Given 1: Do you avoid thinking about your own mortality and the pending death of everyone you love?
  For most of us, the honest answer is, "Yes."

- Given 2: How comfortable are you being alone? Do you need to be in a relationship at all times? Do you have a hard time eating at a restaurant alone? Going to a movie alone? Spending a Friday night alone at home?
  Some of us are not comfortable being alone and will avoid it whenever possible. Others of us find interpersonal relationships so exhausting that we would rather spend our time alone and avoid the vulnerability, work, and emotional connection that intimate relationships require.

- Given 3: To what lengths will you go to feel special and important? Do you tell yourself that the bad things that you see on the news could not happen to you because you are somehow unique? Do you tell yourself, "I wouldn't get sick or be the victim of a crime; That would never happen to me"?
  For most of us, the honest answer is that we believe we are the exception to the rule because we want to be special.

- Given 4: Do you blame your past or other people for your current behavior instead of taking responsibility for it?
  Most of us spend a great deal of time blaming our past for undesirable aspects of ourselves.

- Given 4: How much of yourself do you compromise to feel safe? Do you sacrifice your core values and basic life desires? Do you skirt the truth to make more money? Do you try to control people by demanding that they act a certain way to make you feel secure? Do you ask people whether they miss or love you? Do you try to change people to make yourself more comfortable with your life choices?
  For most of us, the answer is that we will do almost anything to feel safe and secure; we will compromise ourselves emotionally, financially, and spiritually.

All of the Givens combined: Can you say, "I am living an authentic life, driven by my values and beliefs. I am accomplishing all that I am capable of doing and making the most of my time on this planet. If I died tonight, I'd have no regrets or unfinished business."

For most of us, the honest answer is, "No."

Cognitive-Behavioral Perspective

Pioneers in the cognitive-behavioral realms like Aaron Beck and Albert Ellis described how our thoughts are related to our feelings and behavior. They argued that we often think in illogical ways, which leads us to experience irrationally-based emotions and behaviors. However, if we change our thoughts to be more accurate and consistent with reality, our feelings and behavior will also be more realistic.

For example, if I am in a disagreement with my spouse and think to myself, "He [or she] is such a jerk. I am sick of this crap—I want a divorce," I am probably going to feel incredible self-righteous anger and react by storming out of the house, slamming the door on my way out. If I change my thinking to be less extreme and more reasonable, my reaction will change. If I instead think, "I really dislike having these arguments with him/her. It is so hard to negotiate topics that we don't agree on," I am still not going to like having disagreements, but my emotion and behavior will probably be less intense and dramatic.

Some of the most prominent *cognitive distortions* or characteristic thinking errors are listed below. As you read them, think not only about when you use them, but also about how they affect your emotions and your actions.

Polarized Thinking: Lying by thinking in terms of all or nothing, black or white, right or wrong, leaving no room for grey. For example:

- "I will eat no cookies or I will eat the entire box because if I eat one cookie, my diet is ruined. So why not just keep eating?"
- "My day was terrible" or "my day was amazing."
- "You are the most wonderful person I know" or "I hate you."

Emotional Reasoning: Lying by thinking that our feelings accurately reflect reality. For example:

- "I feel hurt, so you must have done something bad to me."
- "I am fat and ugly because I feel fat and ugly."
- "I feel overwhelmed and anxious. My problems must be too big to solve."

Mental filter: Lying by picking out a single negative detail and dwelling on it to the degree that everything becomes negative. For example:

- You had a performance review meeting with your boss last week. Although the overall evaluation was very positive, your boss said that you needed improvement in one specific area. Instead of remembering all of the praise your boss gave you, you only remember the one negative comment he made about the area that needs improvement.
- You got into a fight with your parent last week. You can't stop thinking about it. It is ruining your ability to focus on anything else.
- You put on a pair of pants that usually fit and they were snug in the waist. It ruins your day—everything seems dire and negative.

Overgeneralization: Lying in a way that makes us see a single negative event as an infinite spiral of defeat or failure. For example:
- After going through a bad breakup, you think, "I will never find a fulfilling relationship. I am doomed to be alone."
- After getting denied a promotion at work, you think, "I am never going to be in the place I want in my career."
- After not getting into the college of your dreams, you think, "I am a failure and everyone is going to know it now because I didn't get in."

Fortune-Telling: Lying by believing that our prediction about the future is an already-established fact. We often do this when predicting that something negative will happen. For example:
- "I just started dating this new person but I already know that it isn't going to work. I am always going to struggle in relationships."
- "I have to give a big presentation at work. I know that it is not going to go well."
- "I am never going to be able to eat moderately. I can't do it. It is too hard."

Sociocultural Perspectives

The hardest challenge is to be yourself in a world where everyone is trying to make you be somebody else.

—e. e. cummings

Multicultural and feminist psychologists focus on the ways that cultural contexts influence our development. Pioneers like Derald Sue and Jean Baker Miller argue that cultural norms around sex, race, class, sexual orientation, and a range of other multicultural factors affect our identity because what is deemed normal and abnormal, or desirable and not desirable, is largely culturally determined. For example, living in a racist culture teaches us that being White is better than being non-White. Sexist cultures teach us that being a man is better than being a woman. Homophobist cultures teach us that being straight is better than being gay.

From childhood, we start learning these cultural values. Over time, we consciously and unconsciously internalize these norms and evaluate ourselves (and others) in comparison to them. Consequently, in terms of self-deception, our biggest challenge is to determine whether we aspire to be a certain way because *we believe it is right for us* or because we were *culturally conditioned to believe it was right*. For example, ask yourself the following questions:

- Do you compromise yourself to meet the standards of your culture? For example, do you think you need to get married because society or your religion says you are supposed to? Do you deny that you are homosexual because it would not be accepted? Do you try to fit the mold of what society deems successful instead of following your passion?
  Most of us compromise who we really are in some ways to meet societal standards. Or, we react strongly against societal standards as a mechanism for exploring our identities.

- Do you deny that you have ever had racist thoughts? Sexist thoughts? Homophobic thoughts? Classist thoughts?
  A large body of research suggests that we are conditioned to have such thoughts if we were raised in a patriarchal first-world country, such as the United States, Canada, much of Western Europe, and Australia. Despite that fact, most of us strongly deny it, thereby destroying our ability to change it.

- Do you hold judgmental attitudes toward overweight or obese people, labeling them as stupid, gross, smelly, ugly, lazy, or undisciplined?
  Research suggests that almost all of us living in Western cultural contexts hold anti-fat attitudes, whether we are underweight, average weight, or obese ourselves.

- To what extent did you internalize cultural messages about your gender role, or what is required to be a valuable woman or man in your cultural context?

  Women: Do you aspire to look like the images of women in fashion magazines? Do you criticize your weight and appearance on a daily basis? Does gaining one pound ruin your day? On the flip side, do you hide your "masculine" traits because they are not viewed as positive from a cultural perspective (e.g., your love of hunting, hatred of makeup, and complete disregard for fashion)?

  Men: Do you stop yourself from crying because it is seen as immature and weak? Do you avoid expressing loving emotions to your male friends because it is not acceptable as "one of the guys"? Do you hide your "feminine" traits because they are not viewed positively from a social perspective (e.g., your love of opera and desire to go shopping on Sundays rather than watch football)? Will you only date women that your society deems to be the best looking instead of dating women you find attractive as people?

  The truth is that most of us try to attain the ideal attributes ascribed to our sex by our cultural environment. Such gender-based cultural messages about our value as human beings affect the degree to which we value ourselves and others.

THE COSTS OF SELF-DECEPTION

Unexpressed emotions will never die.
They are buried alive and will come forth later in uglier ways.
—Sigmund Freud

You may be asking yourself, "Why should I care about self-deception? What is the benefit to me?"

Although normative and commonplace, self-deception comes with profound costs. In fact, lying to ourselves may be the most dangerous thing in the world because *we live our truth whether we are honest about it or not.* Our self-deception is exemplified in our thinking patterns, beliefs, behaviors, emotional reactions, and relationships. Anytime our lives are driven by something outside of our awareness, it is dangerous to us and everyone around us.

Hurting Others, Including Those We Love The Most

How people treat others is a direct reflection of how they feel about themselves.
—Unknown

One major cost of self-deception is that we use painful life experiences to justify being non-ideal versions of ourselves. This will directly and indirectly hurt others, especially those we love the most.

All of us have experienced pain in response to challenging life circumstances. Some of our pain may have even been in response to objectively traumatic events; perhaps we were raised by an abusive parent, lost a child, had a near-death experience, were raped, mugged, or became physically disfigured or disabled. In fact, some of the most famous psychologists who laid the groundwork for psychotherapeutic practice experienced tremendous trauma. Both Sigmund Freud and Viktor Frankl were Jews living in Nazi Europe before and during World War II. They watched and experienced human cruelty first-hand in its most extreme form. Freud fled to London before being taken by the Nazis, while Frankl narrowly survived the concentration camps and lost the majority of his family.

When confronted with such hardship, we often justify our emotions, thoughts, and behavior by blaming the situation or other people. For example, we may justify being bitter and angry at men by saying that it is because we were raped. We may justify not trusting people because we were molested by a family friend. We may justify being bitter and mean because we saw the human capacity for evil when the Nazis killed our family.

In these situations, we want to defer responsibility for our reactions. It is very easy for us to do; even reading these examples, many of us can sympathize. However, this response comes at a cost; when we justify who we are by blaming circumstances, we are *lying to ourselves about who is responsible for who we are* and *we will pass our emotional baggage onto others.*

The most obvious example of passing emotional baggage onto others is in the parent-child relationship. Parents often aren't aware or can't acknowledge the direct and indirect effects that their personal struggles have on their children. For example, a mother who is consumed by her own pain may not see that she is completely emotionally unavailable to her child. A father struggling with depression may rely on his child for emotional support without recognizing that it is not the child's job to support him. A mother may claim that the negative comments she makes about her body every time she looks in the mirror don't affect her child. A parent may drink, use drugs, or stay in bed for days feeling depressed without considering that it may be petrifying for a child to watch this happen.

In addition, unhealthy patterns are often passed down from generation to generation. Family systems therapies pioneered by individuals like Alfred Adler, Murray Bowen, and Virginia Satir, propose that dysfunctional patterns of thinking, behavior, and emotions are often trans-generationally communicated. For example, a father may not see that he is abusing his child in exactly the same way that he was abused. A mother may not see that she drinks in response to emotion, as her father did.

The reality is this: Living through difficult life circumstances is not an excuse for passing trauma onto someone else. *We are responsible for ourselves independent of life circumstance.* Our reactions are a reflection of who we are and we are responsible for them *even if what contributed to our pain was objectively horrific and not our fault.* As Victor Frankl wrote about his time in the concentration camps, "The one thing you can't take away from me is the way I choose to respond to what you do to me. The last of one's freedoms is to choose one's attitude in any given circumstance."

Never forget that there are people in the world trying to get over *what you did to them,* just as you are trying to get over what they did to you. The ways in which you lie to yourself not only hurt you—they can cause massive psychological damage to those around you.

Believing And Spreading Our Lies

If you tell a big enough lie and tell it frequently enough, it will be believed.
—Adolf Hitler

Perhaps the most tragic way that self-deception harms us is that we start believing our lies and we teach them to others.

History suggests that we use lies to justify everything from slavery to genocide. We create groups and artificial divisions in our own minds—us versus them—to reinforce that *they* are different from *us* in some fundamental way. They are morally corrupt, not really human, not children of our God, a danger to us. Then we use those differences to justify our choices: *I can now harm them and feel okay about it.*

If we think about extreme acts of cruelty, most of us will deny that we are capable of committing them. We believe that if we had lived in Nazi Germany, we wouldn't have supported Hitler. If we had lived in the 1800s as a White man, we wouldn't have owned slaves. Our self-deception can even lead us to deny what humans are capable of doing to other humans. We would prefer to believe a deluded, flowery version of the truth in which the Holocaust didn't exist and massacres in the Sudan are not currently occurring.

History and a great deal of social psychology research suggests that *we are all capable of acts of cruelty when put in the right environment.* For example, I like to think of myself as a pacifist. But if someone tried to hurt my child, I could hurt that person. If I am really honest with myself, I could kill that person. Ask yourself: If you believed that a group of people were going to destroy you and those you loved, would you support their systematic extermination? History says that we would. And we would justify it by lying to ourselves and spreading those lies to others.

Regret

Regret tomorrow is far worse than honesty today.
—Unknown

The biggest personal cost of self-deception is that it can leave us with massive amounts of regret, both about who we are and about who we could have been.

In addition to hurting those we love the most and disseminating our lies to others, one common reason that we experience regret is that *we made choices with harmful consequences to avoid being honest.* To distract ourselves from the truth, for example, we will do just about anything—we may drink alcohol, use drugs, eat, shop, pick fights, travel, leave, or gamble. Our behavior often reflects the following sentiment, "The truth is too hard to admit. I don't want to face it. So, I am going to distract myself to avoid addressing my core issues." As we avoid the truth, we often create even bigger issues for ourselves and those around us (credit counseling and rehab, here we come!).

We also often experience regret because *we chose not to change.* For example, perhaps you became a doctor or a lawyer because of family pressure even though it wasn't your passion. Perhaps you lost the love of your life because you weren't strong enough to face your fears about intimacy and, as a result, he or she left. Perhaps you seriously harmed others because of your inability to change your abusive behavior. Perhaps you knew that there was another life you could have lived that would have been more fulfilling for you, but you weren't strong enough to make different choices.

Over my years as a therapist, I have worked with a variety of people struggling with a range of problems. Looking back at life with regret is one of the toughest realities to overcome because *you cannot change your choices in the past—only your choices in the present.*

For example, if you ruined your relationships with your children because of the way that you treated them, you have to live with the consequences of that. If you contracted a disease because of sexual promiscuity or drug use, you have to live with that. If you desperately wanted to have children but didn't have them because your partner didn't want them, you have to live with that.

When we aren't honest with ourselves about who we are and what we want, we allow other people and circumstance to determine our life course. We throw away our power. We deny our ability to choose, and we fail to live the life that would have been most fulfilling for us.

PART II: CHOOSING HONESTY

There are two mistakes one can make along the road to truth . . .

not going all the way and not starting.

—Buddha

Anyone who has engaged in psychological work though psychotherapy, self-help practices, or meditation knows that choosing to be honest is incredibly hard. It requires that we develop enough psychological strength and self-esteem to tolerate the truth and to change once the truth is acknowledged.

Unfortunately, our current cultural climate is not going to help us on our journey toward honesty. In the United States (and many other parts of the Western world), we promote the message that unhappiness is inherently bad and should be treated immediately with something that makes us happy. If we feel sad, for example, the media suggests that we should eat chocolate, have a glass of wine, or lose ourselves watching reality television—all to distract ourselves from our own lives.

Additionally, our culture promotes the message that it is better to be nice than to tell the truth. We don't want to tell others our honest opinion if we think it will hurt them or make us look bad.

The truth is that pain is not inherently bad for us; *pain is information*. Sometimes pain is a reasonable reaction to the truth. We would all benefit by shifting our focus from seeing *pain as bad* to seeing *pain as motivation to change*. I am not suggesting that mental illness should not be treated as such. I am also not suggesting that feeling pain is pleasant. However, I am suggesting that to know ourselves requires discomfort—without some anxiety, pain, and discontentment, *we probably will not have sufficient motivation to change*.

In addition to using the information already presented in this book to understand our self-deception, I offer some specific suggestions about how we can start becoming more honest with ourselves in this section. In the short-term, it is very uncomfortable to become more honest with ourselves. In the long-term, however, I fundamentally believe that it is the only way we can live more fulfilling lives. For as we become more honest, we not only feel the pain of our self-deceptive lies; we give ourselves the freedom to make different choices.

Our first step in becoming more honest with ourselves is self-awareness. We start by just noticing—we become *observers of our own lives.*

If we are honest, we are going to learn things that we don't like about ourselves. Our first reaction is going to be that we either become very defensive or highly critical of ourselves or others. *I strongly encourage all of us to suspend any evaluation that may come from increased awareness: do this without judgment or criticism.* Just begin to watch and observe.

As you are observing, ask yourself questions like the following:

- What did I learn in childhood that is influencing my ability to be honest with myself now?

- When do I most often lie to myself? About what?

- When I lie, what is it that triggers my discomfort? For example, am I uncomfortable around beautiful women? Rich men? Single people? Kids? Siblings? Religious people? If so, why?

- What psychological strategies do I use most often to lie? For example, which ego-defense mechanisms do I use the most (denial, projection, regression)? What existential Givens of Life do I avoid confronting? What cognitive thinking errors do I use most often? What social messages have I internalized as relevant that may not serve me well?

As we become more introspective about our own lives, it will be particularly hard to be honest about two themes: 1) things that we learned in childhood that are deeply rooted in our identity development and 2) topics that are most socially taboo (such as racism, classism, ageism, and homophobia). To help us become more honest, particularly in these areas, we need to pay attention to our emotions, behavior, and thoughts.

Notice Your Emotion. When we have a strong emotional reaction to something, it is an amazing opportunity to understand ourselves better. *Pause.* Ask yourself:

- What is this emotion? Can I identify it? Can I admit it? Is it embarrassment? Shame? Sadness? Resentment? Anger? Anxiety?

- Where is the emotion coming from? What triggered this feeling in me?
- What does this feeling remind me of? Is it reminiscent of something I felt as a child? Does it occur around specific types of people or in certain environmental circumstances?

Our emotions will give us a great deal of information about what is hard for us to admit, which will lead us back to our self-deceptive tendencies. We need to see our emotions as a reflection of who we are in some way.

Notice Your Behavior. We desperately want to separate *our identity from our behavior*. We don't really want our behavior to be a reflection of who we are. For example:

- We want to have a few drinks and then drive home, but not be drunk drivers.
- We want to be able to swear at our kids, but be good parents.
- We want to ask others if they love/miss/want/need us in an emotionally desperate moment, but not be needy.
- We want to be able to have random sexual encounters, but not be promiscuous.
- We want to tell a racist joke, but not be racist.
- We want to have dramatic emotional outbursts in which we destroy someone else's character, but not be emotionally abusive.

The truth is that *the way we act is a direct reflection of who we are in some way.* When what we say doesn't match how we act, we are lying to ourselves. Ask yourself:

- What does my behavior say about me?
- What do I not want to admit to myself about my behavior?
- What insecurities are motivating my behavior?
- What do I need to change about my behavior to feel better about who I am?

Notice Your Thoughts. We like to think that our thoughts are actually truth—that they accurately reflect reality. The truth is that our thoughts are *not an accurate reflection of reality*—they are often incredibly biased, skewed, and inaccurate in characteristic ways that harm our ability to be honest. Ask yourself:

- What words do I use to describe myself and others?

- What cognitive thinking errors do I use most often?
- How am I using my past to justify my current thinking?
- What negative attitudes and judgmental thoughts do I have about myself and others?

As suggested by our cognitive-behavioral experts, our thoughts will be directly related to the way that we feel and behave. As we examine our thinking patterns, we must also consider how our thoughts interact with our feelings and behaviors in damaging ways.

USING OUR RELATIONSHIPS

Holding onto anger is like drinking poison and expecting the other person to die.
—Buddha

Most of us spend a huge amount of energy trying to get over *someone or something that happened to us*: a traumatic childhood, poor parenting, a bad breakup, or challenging relationships with family, friends, and romantic partners. Even I encouraged you to examine your past in the beginning of this book as a means of self-exploration because your past has fundamentally influenced who you are today and where you will be most vulnerable to lying.

That said, I believe that we must always look at relationships from two perspectives: what the other person brings to the table and what we bring to the table. Most of us can easily do the former—we can all rattle off a laundry list of descriptors for our parents, family, and friends. The latter, however, is much harder for most of us to do because we generally avoid examining *our contribution to aspects of ourselves and our lives that we do not like*.

So, before you say what you don't like about someone or what that person did to you, ask yourself this: *What does my reaction to this person say about me?* Take the finger we often use to point out another person's "flaws" and point it at yourself. Ask yourself:

- Does this person bring out my insecurities in some way? Am I embarrassed or ashamed to be around him or her? Am I somehow afraid of this person? Am I judgmental? Angry or holding onto resentment?

- Does he or she remind me of something about myself that I don't like?

- Does he or she remind me of my parent or my past?

- What can I learn about myself from this person? What can he or she teach me about who I am and how I need to change?

- How have I affected this person? Have I passed on painful experiences to this person?

- When have I torn down someone else—a partner, child, flight attendant, customer service agent—to make myself feel better? What is it about that person or situation that led me to react by criticizing someone else?

When we use our relationships as a mechanism for self-reflection and increased awareness, we can learn a great deal about who we really are and where we lie to ourselves the most.

I also believe that there is a gift in every relationship. Whether it is challenging or easy, every relationship we have is an opportunity to explore ourselves.

CHOICE AND RESPONSIBILITY

Between stimulus and response there is a space. In that space is our power to choose our response. In our response lies our growth and our freedom.

—*Viktor Frankl*

Choice is everything. Through self-awareness, we increase our power to choose and freedom to change. However, with self-awareness comes responsibility. As we understand ourselves, we are now more responsible for our choices because we *have the freedom to change or to stay the same once we admit the truth.*

All of us know what it feels like to see something about ourselves that we don't like and not change—especially because in these moments, our self-deceptive nature kicks into full gear so that we can re-convince ourselves that we don't need to change. These are generally moments in life when we look back on our choices saying, "I knew better: I saw it, I felt it, I have been here before and I promised myself I wouldn't do it again. Yet, here I am, and I did it again. And I feel terrible about it." For example:

- I said I wasn't going to get drunk and drive home anymore. Last night I did.

- I know that I have a gambling problem. I promised myself that I wouldn't go to the casino, but I did it anyway.

- I promised myself that I wouldn't repeatedly call my partner in moments of panic to get reassurance and comfort. I know I need to stop doing that because my partner cannot "fix" my feelings, which are coming from my past. But last night I was feeling particularly vulnerable and I called twenty-five times in a row because he/she wouldn't answer the phone. I knew better. Now, not only do I have to deal with the reason I felt panic in the first place, but I also have to clean up the mess I created in my relationship.

- I said that I wasn't going to go on shopping sprees that I cannot afford. Yesterday I was out with a friend. I felt insecure around him/her and, to cope with my feelings, I spent my entire month's rent on stuff that I don't need. At the time, I knew that I was shopping to cover up the fact that I felt insecure because I think this person is very good looking and has more money than I do. But I couldn't stop myself from buying things. I acted like I could afford it, even though I can't.

- I promised myself that I would not make negative comments about my eating or physical appearance in front of my daughter. Yesterday I did and I saw the look on her face. It is not okay.

When we choose to acknowledge that something negative about us is true but we don't change it, we are *more responsible for the consequences than before we acknowledged the truth.* Psychologically, it will hurt us more: In this way, ignorance really is bliss.

I want to take a moment to specifically address our choices and responsibility for the little people in our lives. Whether we are parents, aunts or uncles, teachers, mentors, or grandparents, children offer us one of our biggest opportunities to change because they often bring out our biggest insecurities. For example, when we are around children, we may be reminded of pain from our own childhood. We may react personally to a child's behavior, such as feeling jealous when a child acknowledges closeness to other people (e.g., a babysitter, a teacher, another parent or step-parent). We may even react to a child's perception of the world, such as telling a child that he is wrong when he tells us that we are being unfair or mean in some way.

In addition to bringing out our insecurities, children are highly affected by us in a formative, identity-based way. Consequently, our relationships to children are ripe with the potential for dysfunction. Adults are more sensitive and reactive while children are easily influenced and damaged. Given these realities, *it is critical that we take extra responsibility for the choices we make around children because we may be teaching them something fundamental about themselves, us, and the world.*

At the most basic level, our job description as caregivers is to do what is in the best interest of the children in our lives 100 percent of the time. We cannot let ourselves pass down our baggage to children; we need to hold ourselves accountable for what we teach them. When you are around children, ask yourself, "Am I communicating my issues to this child through my words, non-verbal communication, or emotional reactions in some way?" If the answer is, "Yes," *stop yourself dead in your tracks. This is not the child's problem.* If we are passing our baggage onto children, we must take immediate steps to behave in ways that we believe to be in the best interest of the child. Our job is to meet their needs—it is not their job to meet ours.

In the same vein, the children in our lives don't owe us anything. If they like us and want to spend time with us, that is amazing. Be grateful, but don't think that you are entitled to it.

As we take greater responsibility for ourselves and our choices, the hope is that we will continue to evolve into a better version of ourselves. Consistent with that theme, I encourage us to handle challenging situations and people with grace; to be contented with how we handled ourselves in every life situation; and to develop enough psychological strength to apologize for our roles in the creation of our own problems. *Although we cannot control many of the circumstances we encounter in life, we are responsible for our responses to all of them.*

Psychology cannot tell people how they ought to live their lives. It can, however, provide them with the means for effective personal and social change.

—Albert Bandura

Self-awareness is necessary but insufficient to living a fulfilling life. Getting honest with ourselves demands action.

As we learn about ourselves, we have to do something with the information we learn or it will actually end up hurting us more over time. If we don't change, we will pay the price of knowing that we have a problem and are not doing anything about it—and that will be our own fault. For example:

- If you admit that you are insecure around "beautiful people," you now have to work on your insecurity (or pay the psychological price of knowing the truth but not changing).

- If you admit that you have a problem with drugs or alcohol, you now have to confront the reasons that you use and challenge yourself to stop.

- If you admit that you communicate your insecurities to your children in a damaging way, you now have to change it.

- If you admit that you eat to cope with unpleasant emotions, you now have to learn to deal with your emotions in another way.

There are times in our lives when we begin to get honest with ourselves but are not willing to do anything differently. As described by James Prochaska and James Norcross, when we acknowledge that we want our lives to be different in some way, we will fall somewhere on a continuum between *not at all ready to change my life* and *I will do anything to change my life.*

When we find ourselves in a position in which we learn the truth and choose not to change, *it is psychologically healthier for us to admit the truth and our reason for not doing anything about it.* For example:

I am unhappily married but choose to stay with my partner because:
- I am afraid to leave.
- I don't want to be alone.
- I don't know how I would support myself.
- I believe that it is better for my children to have married parents than to have

divorced parents.

I hate my job but I won't quit because:

- I don't know anything else.
- I am afraid of the unknown.
- I am not qualified to do anything else and I am not willing to go back to school to train to do a job that I would love.

I want to lose weight but don't because:

- I won't exercise.
- I don't like to diet. Sometimes I spend a few days eating really well but then I give up because it doesn't seem to make a difference quickly enough.
- I feel terribly about myself, and to lose weight would require that I confront how I got to be this heavy to begin with.
- I won't make the time to care for my own health.
- I like chocolate, cookies, and ice cream too much to eat them moderately.

When we choose not to change in spite of the truth, it is in our best interest to take full responsibility for our choice while continuing to acknowledge the truth. Try to embrace the following sentiment:

"I am miserable. I am now more aware of why I am miserable and what it would take for me to be happier. However, I am not willing to do it. Consequently, I am not going to allow myself to speak negatively about my reality anymore. Instead, I am going to acknowledge that all of this is true, embrace the life that I have, and find a way to be as fulfilled as possible with the exact reality of my life as it exists today."

Starting now, when you won't change, do not allow yourself to complain about being miserable, either to yourself or to other people. When you are honest with yourself but won't change, that is a choice. If you are not going to change, try to become happy with who you are and what you have.

That said, there is no time like the present. You always have a choice. You can choose to change starting in this exact moment, today.

FIND A GREAT THERAPIST

If you tell the truth, it becomes a part of your past.
If you lie, it becomes a part of your future.
—Unknown

Social stigma exists around mental illness and psychotherapy. People frequently say things like "I don't need therapy—it is only for crazy or weak people who can't help themselves. I was in therapy as a kid and it didn't help at all, so I don't believe that it works anyway." You may even say these things to yourself.

I believe the exact opposite—it takes tremendous courage and strength to open up and be completely vulnerable to another person. Working with a great therapist is incredibly hard work, in large part because it helps us become honest with ourselves. It is much easier for us to avoid confronting our self-deception than to tackle it head-on.

The truth is that psychotherapy is probably the *only relationship you will ever have in our entire life that exists solely to benefit you.* That is truly a gift if you are courageous enough to accept it.

In practical terms, finding a great therapist is like finding any other medical professional—it is about finding a good fit for you. If you begin therapy and don't feel a connection to the therapist, I suggest you try another. Don't give up if the first therapist you see doesn't seem right for you. That said, a great therapist will often tell you things that you don't want to hear and make you incredibly uncomfortable. That is *not* a good reason to find another therapist—in fact, that is probably the best reason to stay with the one that you have.

When we begin to get honest with ourselves, we feel uncomfortable. And we are confronted with a choice—to change or not to change. The more honest we are with ourselves, the more responsible we are for our choice.

I end with a personal story of understanding myself and choosing honesty. I was on the perfect path to be a successful academic. I earned my doctorate in clinical psychology training under some fantastic mentors at some very reputable institutions. I received tenure at the University of Nevada, Las Vegas (UNLV) at thirty-three years old. And two years later, I resigned.

For any of you who know something about academia, getting tenure and then quitting is about the last thing anyone would expect from a faculty member. My career and personal life were a carefully constructed exercise in trying to please people, feel safe, and do the right thing. And it benefitted me greatly. I love psychology. I love education. I love my students. I love UNLV. I value all of these things greatly: they helped make me who I am today.

After getting tenure, I had a baby. I started thinking about my life and how I really wanted to live it. As it was laid out, I would spend the next thirty years of my life running a successful research lab and advancing our understanding of eating pathology and cultural competency by publishing articles in peer-reviewed journals written for other psychologists.

And the truth is, *that sounded terrible.* I wanted to spend more time with my daughter. And I wanted to help people who would benefit most from our research but who rarely have access to that information—the general public. Getting myself to admit that was *brutally painful.* I had to confront all of my self-deceptive lies and insecurities. It challenged my sense of safety and security, my loyalty to those who trained me, and my identity as a scholar and expert in the field. My mind raced with questions like: What if I disappoint people? What will my family say? What about my department, my mentors, and my profession—am I letting everyone down? What if I can't support myself? Who am I if I am not a professor and researcher? What will my professional identity be? *What if my whole life changes!* What if my whole life *doesn't* change?

I am telling you this because I had to be honest with myself—being a professor wasn't my path anymore. I wanted something else. When you get honest with yourself, you can't take the information back. You actually *must* take action. *This does not mean that your past was a mistake.* In fact, I wouldn't be who I am today without having gone through this process.

That said, if I had admitted that I didn't want to be a professor anymore and *still chosen to stay in academia* to feed my insecurities and self-deceptive lies, I would have paid a price—a huge psychological price that would have left me with a great deal of regret. For someday, I would have had to admit that the reason I lived my life the way I did was not because it was what I wanted. It was because I was not strong enough to make different choices when confronted with the truth about what I needed *to live a fulfilling life for me.*

Fighting our self-deception is a lifelong journey. We will not wake up one morning and say, "I am done! I know everything about myself. I am a fully honest person with no self-deception." As we grow, the world will offer us new ways to understand the more evolved version of ourselves and present us with more opportunities to change.

The best way to look back on our lives with no regret is to live authentically in the present, one day at a time. When we choose to be more honest about our self-deception, we will be able to say, "I made the best choices I could with the information I had each day of my life." That is as good as it is going to get.

Choose honesty, now. I am doing the same.

As the child of two college professors, Cortney was raised in an academic environment. In addition to attaining a formal education in the classroom, she traveled extensively, getting a "real-world" education. Before the age of twenty, Cortney had lived in Australia and Argentina and traveled throughout Central America, South America, Russia, Scandinavia, and Western Europe. Exposed to a diversity of cultures and lifestyles from an early age, she was intrigued by the ways cultural and environmental conditions affected the psychological well-being of individuals, groups, and even entire societies.

Her interest in psychology and issues of cultural diversity took academic shape as an undergraduate at Macalester College in St. Paul, Minnesota. Under the exceptional mentorship of Drs. Jaine Strauss (Macalester College) and Nancy C. Raymond (University of Minnesota), Cortney developed a strong interest in the cultural components of eating disorders, and undertook supporting research and clinical activities.

After graduating magna cum laude from Macalester, Cortney entered the doctoral program in clinical psychology at Texas A&M University to work under the mentorship of Drs. David H. Gleaves and Antonio Cepeda-Benito, who specialize in cross-cultural and linguistic issues in the assessment and treatment of eating disorders. From there, she completed her predoctoral clinical internship at McLean Hospital/Harvard Medical School and joined the faculty at the University of Nevada, Las Vegas (UNLV) in 2006.

Through her formal and informal learning experiences, Cortney saw the ways in which we lie to ourselves on a daily basis and the danger that it posed to our emotional well-being. Helping people understand themselves and see their own self-deception became a fundamental part of her clinical practice, research, teaching, and personal way of life.

Although Cortney received tenure at UNLV in 2012, she formally retired from academia in 2014 to pursue a career that would allow her more time with her family and more interaction with the general public. As Cortney moves into a new phase of her career, she hopes to use psychological research and clinical observations to help the public live more fulfilling lives by confronting their self-deception. In addition to doing this generally, Cortney plans to address how self-deception contributes to unhealthy eating behavior and negative body image.

For more information on Cortney's work:

www.choosehonesty.com

cortneywarren@choosehonesty.com

The information described in this book is a combination of years of formal schooling, clinical observations, and personal life experience. As such, it is difficult to accurately and adequately acknowledge the countless researchers and theorists whose writings have influenced me and, consequently, the content of this book. This is especially true of the scholarly work of such pioneers in Psychology as Sigmund Freud, Carl Jung, and Viktor Frankl. Given the extensive nature of their scholarship as some of the founders of this field, there simply is no one book or article to cite here that reflects their contributions to my understanding of the theory and practice of psychology, as expressed in this book.

What follows is a very selective list of references that specifically address issues and positions provided in this book:

American Psychological Association (2003). "Guidelines on multicultural education, training, research, practice, and organizational change for psychologists." American Psychologist, 58, 377–402.

American Psychological Association (2009). "Guidelines for psychological practice with girls and women." American Psychologist, 62, 979–979.

Edited by Barlow, David H. (2001). Clinical Handbook of Psychological Disorders (Third edition). New York, NY: The Guilford Press.

Beck, Aaron T. (1975). Cognitive Therapy and the Emotional Disorders. Madison, CT: International Universities Press, Inc.

Brumberg, J. (1997). The Body Project: An Intimate History of American Girls. New York, NY: Random House Inc.

Burns, David. D. (1980). Feeling Good: The New Mood Therapy. New York, NY: A Signet Book New American Library.

Corey, G. (2009). Theory and Practice of Counseling and Psychotherapy (Eighth Edition). Pacific Grove, CA: Brooks/Cole.

Ellis, Albert and Harper, Robert A. (1975). A Guide to Rational Living (Third Edition). Chatsworth, CA: Wilshire Book Company.

Frankl, Viktor (1963). Man's Search for Meaning. Boston, MA: Beacon Press.

Freud, Sigmund S. (1995). The Basic Writings of Sigmund Freud. Translated and edited by A. A. Brill. New York, NY: Random House, Inc.

Freud, Sigmund S. (1936). The Ego and the Mechanisms of Defense. New York, NY: International Universities Press.

Freud, Sigmund S. (1960). The Ego and the Id. Translated by Joan Riviere, Revised and edited by James Strachey. New York, NY: W. W. Norton & Company Inc.

Editors Gurman, Alan S. and Messer, Stanley B. (2003). Essential Psychotherapies: Theory and Practice (Second Edition). New York, NY: The Guilford Press.

Editors Hubble, Mark A., Duncan, Barry L., and Miller, Scott D. (1999). The Heart & Soul of Change: What Works in Therapy. Washington, DC: American Psychological Association.

Jung, Carl G. (1933). Modern Man in Search of a Soul. Translated by W. S. Dell and Cary F. Baynes. New York, NY: Houghton Mifflin Harcourt Inc.

Jung, Carl G. (1959). The Basic Writings of C. G. Jung, edited by V. S. de Laszlo. New York, NY: The Modern Library.

McWilliams, Nancy (2011). Psychoanalytic Diagnosis: Understanding Personality Structure in the Clinical Process (Second Edition). New York, NY: The Guilford Press.

Minuchen, Salvador (1974). Families & Family Therapy. Cambridge, MA: Harvard University Press.

Myss, Caroline (2009). Defy Gravity: Healing Beyond the Bounds of Reason. Carlsbad, CA: Hay House Inc.

Rogers, Carl (1961). On Becoming a Person: A Therapist's View of Psychotherapy. Boston, MA: Houghton Mifflin Paperback.

Sue, D. W. & Sue, D. (2013). Counseling The Culturally Diverse: Theory And Practice (6th ed.). New York, NY: John Wiley & Sons.

Thompson, J. Kevin, Heinberg, Leslie J., Altabe, Madeline, & Tantleff-Dunn, Stacey (1999). Exacting beauty: Theory, Assessment, and Treatment of Body Image Disturbance. Washington, DC: American Psychological Association.

Yalom, Irvin D. (1995). The Theory and Practice of Group Psychotherapy (Fourth Edition). New York, NY: Basic Books.

Yalom, I. D. (2000). Love's Executioner and Other Tales of Psychotherapy. New York, NY: Perennial Classics.

Printed in Great Britain
by Amazon

21440646R00031